God's Princess

A Reminder of Whose You Are
As You Navigate This World

Tawonga Nyangulu

Trilogy Christian Publishers
A Wholly Owned Subsidiary of Trinity Broadcasting Network
2442 Michelle Drive
Tustin, CA 92780

Copyright © 2021 by Tawonga Nyangulu

All Scripture quotations, unless otherwise noted, taken from THE HOLY BIBLE, NEW INTERNATIONAL VERSION®, NIV® Copyright © 1973, 1978, 1984, 2011 by Biblica, Inc.® Used by permission. All rights reserved worldwide.

Scripture quotations marked (KJV) taken from *The Holy Bible, King James Version*. Cambridge Edition: 1769.

All rights reserved, including the right to reproduce this book or portions thereof in any form whatsoever.

Cover design by: Cornerstone Creative Solutions

For information, address Trilogy Christian Publishing
Rights Department, 2442 Michelle Drive, Tustin, Ca 92780.
Trilogy Christian Publishing/ TBN and colophon are trademarks of Trinity Broadcasting Network.

For information about special discounts for bulk purchases, please contact Trilogy Christian Publishing.

Manufactured in the United States of America

Trilogy Disclaimer: The views and content expressed in this book are those of the author and may not necessarily reflect the views and doctrine of Trilogy Christian Publishing or the Trinity Broadcasting Network.

10 9 8 7 6 5 4 3 2 1

Library of Congress Cataloging-in-Publication Data is available.

ISBN 978-1-64773-696-5 (Print Book)
ISBN 978-1-64773-697-2 (ebook)

This book is dedicated to my beautiful Zahra. May you always remember how highly your creator thinks of you. You are His princess.

Love always,
Mom

You Are Loved

When the world seems silent
And you feel alone
Remember to look up
To the Great God

He thinks the world of you
He calls you His friend
He created you wonderfully and fearfully
Every little detail on your body is in its intended place
Beautiful, just the way you are
He makes no mistakes
He thinks the world of you

He loves you so greatly
He loves you so very well
He never leaves you
He is right there with you
Always with you

Look up verse: Psalm 139:14

Write your thoughts here:

You Are A Leader

When the world calls you bossy
Remember He who created you
Thinks so very highly of you
You were created to lead

He calls you royalty
He calls you precious
He calls you the head
He says you are a leader
He says you are special to Him
You are his precious daughter

Look up verse: 1 Peter 2:9

Write your thoughts here:

You Are Protected

When you feel afraid
And it feels like the world is caving in on you
Remember the one who watches over you does not slumber or sleep
You are the apple of his eye
His eye is always on you
He sends his angels to watch over you

Look up verse: Psalm 91:11

Write your thoughts here:

Your Prayers Are Heard

When life seems tough
Remember the one who parted the Red Sea
Is the same God you serve today
The same God who made water come out of a rock
Is available to you today
He does not change
He is the same yesterday, today, and forever
He did it before and He can do it again
His power has not changed
He says that if you ask you will receive
So talk to Him boldly
Ask Him anything
He is always listening

Look up verse: Hebrews 13:8

Write your thoughts here:

You Have Authority

When you feel helpless
Remember there is power in your tongue
Your God has given you authority
The wind and waves obey him
He tells you to speak to the mountains
And they must obey you and fall into the sea
You have more power than you think you

Look up verse: Matthew 21:21

Write your thoughts here:

You Are Healed

When you are sick
Remember that Jesus was whipped so that you can be well
In his pain lies your healing
He took all sickness and the pain
So that we do not have to be sick and in pain
By His stripes you are healed
Say out loud to yourself
"By the stripes of Jesus, I am healed."

Look up verse: I Peter 2:24

Write your thoughts here:

You Are Cared For

When you feel overwhelmed
Remember to give your cares to Him
His love for you is never ending
He cares about every little thing that concerns you
He knows about every single thing that bothers you
Trust that you can come boldly before him
You can tell him anything and everything
Pour out your heart to Him
He hears you when you pray

Look up verse: 1 Peter 5:7

Write your thoughts here:

You Are Never Alone

When you feel left out
Remember God does not leave you out
He is always there with you
He has said he will never leave us
He keeps his word

Look up verse: Deuteronomy 31:6

Write your thoughts here:

You Are Strong

When you feel weak
Remember you are strong
The word of God calls you strong
Ask God to help you
He will give you strength

Look up verse: Isaiah 40:29

Write your thoughts here:

You Matter

When people do not like you
Remember the one who made you makes no mistakes
You are just right exactly the way you are
Before you were even born
God already created you carefully
In your mother's tummy
He knows everything about you
He loves you and you matter more to Him than anything
There is absolutely nothing you can do
To change God's love for you

Look up verse: Jeremiah 1:5

Write your thoughts here:

You Are Human And So You Will Make Mistakes

When you have been mean to others
Make sure to run to your creator God
He who made you knows how to get you right again
In life we all make mistakes
Just remember to ask Him for forgiveness
His arms are always wide open
Nothing can change His love for you
He loves you unconditionally
Run to Him for forgiveness

Psalm 51:1–2

Write your thoughts here:

You Can Have Stability In God

When life is unstable

Remember God does not change

He is the one thing that is constant and will be constant

Life may be full of changes

It may sometimes feel like a roller coaster

Sometimes it goes up

Sometimes it goes down

Sometimes things happen that make you happy

Sometimes things happen that make you sad

But through it all, God is the same

Do not let anything move you away from your loving God

Look up verse: Romans 8:38-39

Write your thoughts here:

You Can Have God's Peace

When your mind is racing
Remember that Jesus gives you peace
Think about Him all the time
Shift your thoughts towards Him
Ask Him to give you peace
He will keep you in perfect peace
Because your mind is focused on him

Isaiah 26:3

Write your thoughts here:

You Can Have God's Wisdom

When you don't know what to do
You can always ask God who gives wisdom
There once lived a king called Solomon
He asked God for wisdom
In return God gave him wisdom, riches, and so much more
God always knows what we need
He always knows what we want
He always knows what we should do
Ask Him for wisdom
He will freely give it to you
And show you the right way

Look up verse: James 1:5

You Have God's Provision

When you need something but cannot afford it
Remember to ask God
He is your provider
He is the maker of all things
He is a rich God
He is your king
You are His princess
He knows what you want
He knows what you need
He cares about everything that happens in your life
Ask Him to supply all your needs
He is able to supply everything you need

Look up verse: Philippians 4:19

Write your thoughts here:

You Can Be A Giver

When someone you know is in need
Think of all that you have been blessed with
Think about how you can give to help
You might just be the answer to someone's prayer
It is such a blessing to give
You will never run out of blessings when you give

Look up verse: Luke 6:38

Write your thoughts here:

You Are Excellent

When the voice of the world seems louder
Steal away to a quiet place
Nothing feels better than pleasing the one who created you
Do not give in to the world's ways

The world will try to tell you how you should speak
The world will try to tell how you should eat
The world will try to tell you how you should dress
The world will try to tell you how you should look
The world will try to tell you to compromise

When you quiet yourself you will hear His voice
He says you were created in his image
Be confident in how you were created
Be sure to care for your body because it is the image of God
Dress the way He says you should
Feed your body the way He says you should
Love yourself the way He says you should

Do not let any voice be bigger than God's voice
You are blessed beyond measure
You are excellent

Look up verse: Daniel 6:3

Write your thoughts here:

You Have A Bright Future

When you feel like you are not enough
Remember you are so very enough
Before you were born, God knew you
He knew every single thing you were going to do
Nothing surprises him
He already has good plans for your life
So remember to speak to yourself with kind words
Take comfort in knowing that God has ordered your steps
He has good plans for your life

Look up verse: Jeremiah 29:11

You Can Do Anything

When you are faced with a challenge
Know that God is with you even right in the middle of the challenge
He knows what you are going through
Nothing takes him by surprise
He has already made a way out
With His help you can do anything

Look up verse: Philippians 4:13

Write your thoughts here:

You Should Forgive

When someone upsets you
Remember to always forgive
God's word tells us to be kind
There will always be people who do not like you
There will always be people who make you angry
There will always be people who irritate you
Don't let them have control over your happiness
Don't let your anger last all day
Always forgive and let go

Look up verse: Ephesians 4:26

Write your thoughts here:

About the Author

Tawonga Nyangulu was born and raised in Malawi, Africa. She has a passion for mentoring young women. She lives in Dallas, Texas with her husband and ten-year-old daughter.

CPSIA information can be obtained
at www.ICGtesting.com
Printed in the USA
LVHW021222240621
691048LV00008B/240